Killing Things

KILLING THINGS

John Degen

Acknowledgements
The publisher wishes to thank the Canada Council for the Arts, the Ontario Arts Council and individual patrons for their ongoing support of our publishing program.

Edited for the press by Kevin Connolly

CANADIAN CATALOGUING IN PUBLICATION DATA

Degen, John
    Killing things

Poems
ISBN 0-9686522-8-X

I. Toronto (Ont.) — Poetry. II. Title

PS8557.E368K54 2002   C811'.6   C2002-900400-4
PR9199.3.D429K54 2002

First Edition

Cover Photo Julius Degen (Hartwig Degen, Lake Simcoe 1965)

Inside Photos Peggy Degen

Design Zab Design & Typography

Printed in Canada

this book is dedicated to my parents,
Peggy and Julius Degen

Killing Things

CONTENTS

Things that kill

A deadly physics

The 400 series poems

Things that kill

GOLD STONE NOODLE RESTAURANT

Tuesday mornings on St. Andrew Street,
a truck idles, stacked twelve high
with live chickens; when it rains,
you smell chickens through your skin.

A block away, on Augusta
men stack opaque five-gallon buckets
marked liquid whole egg.
How many accidental bits of shell
in a golden swamp,
how many perfect, unbroken surprises?

Spadina is readying under stone lions
and a widening sky —
smoking boys scrape the walk
to arrange crates of asian pear, navel orange
and sweet, netted durian.

I will smile at the noodle man
each day until he smiles back.
His window shows a new
smoked pig every morning.

We are all awake and hungry.
There are shoes everywhere.

NEIGHBOURS ARE DANGEROUS

They are shooting old women
in the flower gardens, hanging
children like Christmas lights.

I recommend isolation,
hiding and not answering
when called for.

There is merit in broadening
your appetite to rotted things,
the papery bark of softer trees.

Remove anything yellow
and believe it is wonderful
to sleep in rivers.

It is the alternatives now
that comfort, the livers
of wild hares, the breath of housecats

you steal for warmth, a dirt
blanket, and the happy knowledge
there is nothing uglier
than what you are.

SIBELIUS PARK

One

At night in winter,
dead cold
             presumably
a young girl is torn and left
to darken the snow.

The night train ambling through,
sway-hipped, witnesses locked gates,
trodden snow under street lamps,
bare streets, a half halo
of yellow light at the station.

To read the town now
is to trip into sleep
over a clumsy story
of quick fear, indifference
and the slow squeezing
of blood from the lungs.

Two

Today in Sibelius Park, a boy
balances in the crotch of a tree,
hooking down a frisbee, with
the toothpick blade of a hockey stick.

This is a city full of girls becoming
women, and one or two not;
like a story
talked down through years
beneath gabled roofs
and behind the cracked glass
of hundred-year-old windows;
girls watching the city in a swirl
of hands and pointing;
girls alone with their lemonade.

Three

Today Sibelius Park
is an ozone jar,
a column of breathing
in hot, yellow Toronto.

Dogs are brought here in cars
to run and smell and
rinse the roads clean with their tongues,
to filter the park
with their lungs.

Today Sibelius Park hacks out
the city — sick
with experience,
the hands of wandering killers
in fragrant clusters
behind the ornamental fence.

In thirty years of the old
dormancy, verdancy,
it has lost a claim to purity,
hippy poets wrestling their gods,
the hissing of summer lawns,
time unmetered by liquid clocks.

Today the park forgets
its girl.

A GIRL I DON'T KNOW

I'm kissing a
girl on a rooftop
above Queen Street,
a kiss of pure success,

the result of real work,
climbing stairs,
asking names,
turning corners in safety,
then walking back
out of it.

Queen Street flows
its Saturday flow,
late and tired but very
good looking.

She makes me think of
creatures I've never seen,
things with stronger eyes
and webbing in places,
not entirely alive.

I want to forget about the
cat-shaped clock in
her kitchen,
the bright, bright bulb
above the toilet, a glimpse
of violet underwear
over the palest of
skin, that feeling
of being Irish, and
sudden crying.

I will walk a long
way, still able to see
her in the window,
her hands at her face;
the darkness helping
to keep everything in that tunnel
between this road
and her living room, still lit,
still inviting,
and she with her hand
still at her mouth; a distance
now I'll have to pay
attention to

between the two of us
on her bicycle, ridiculous
down Bathurst,
only a matter of hours
till the sickness comes
and sets me shaking
on the couch.

I am in the middle of the road,
remembering her bicycle
and then I am circled,
alone on asphalt
still hot from a
hot day.

A young man on
a bicycle performs
a quiet, imperfect ring,
eyes on my eyes,

an assessment, a threat-squint
unmistakable, looking
for weakness, stopping
and restarting time.

His tires make an empty
noise, the sound
of air surrounded,
and I show him
my defeat,
empty my pockets
inside his circle.

For him,
I am empty of challenge,
the centre of nothing,
a success.

ROSSETTI AT DINNER

Later, I try to explain about water;

if you pay attention over half a life,
you feel when it begins
to be a bad idea.

I say, sky and water
stare at each other
until they decide an outcome,

        the ocean spreads fingers around Long Island,
        and rakes for loose people,

a swell differs from a wave
in purpose as well as style.

The man who takes his Bloody Mary
outdoors and watches the harbour
descend black orange into night,
        to make sure of things,
will always know more about water
than I do.

Rossetti pours an oyster past his tongue,
short-fingered hands on the bar
making an end of the event;
        an agreement.

A rough sea
means one more fine dinner,

       means the trees will smell
       more like themselves to me
       for a time.

He says fighting the current back into
a sheltered bay
       means this time only.

BLANCA ON LONG ISLAND

Her soup contains all the bones
of the animal; translated,
she hides nothing, and
her laughter is earned.

When she walks to look
at the ducks, there are
ducks waiting.
The ocean wonders
at her distance.

At home on two shores,
she faces herself when she
meets a beach,
and must look out across water
for children and aging friends.

In winter, the town empties
of film stars, and reads
her small form, walking,
a poem

FEBRUARY 14, 2001

This day should carry
a superstition
to drive lovers into
dark rooms out of
reach of one another,

the card delivered too late
to change her mind,
the poor-taste souvenir,
half a conversation never received.

One should run at the suggestion
of kisses on this day,
cover one's mouth in
cold-sore lotion, and drink
camphor to discourage intimacy —
something green
to colour the tongue.

A time to remember small
infidelities, one's own mostly,
pained movements on the
hinge of decision,
to say

of course, it might
have been so different;
it could very well
have gone better;
maybe if I'd worn
a nicer shirt.

Think of all the subway flowers,
pity signatures, untouched
breasts.

This is a day to read
books on solitude,
by widowers learning to garden
and women who have
lost lovers in war
after only just finding them,
a day to remove
something and not replace it.

Beware of restaurants
and taxicabs today;
they are not real, but
will seem to be, in stories,
later on
when you are not annoyed
at his socks,
and she has not thrown up
in public, from too much wine
and humiliation.

CERTAIN FAILURES

Across the harbour
the planes touch down
every couple of minutes,
like they're trying to prove something;
circling wide
over the islands and dropping
fast, with the city beside them
as audience.
These are city people in small planes,
phones to their ears, and they are
trying to prove something.

We are drinking beer, Scott and I,
one every couple of minutes
in a café on the harbour,
and our friendship is set
in these moments of anticipation, the few
seconds we know each plane
won't make it.
We lay bets on the lives of these city people,
winning and losing equally, taking
turns playing stooge,
all debts paid in beer,
as has always been our arrangement.

"That one," he says, pointing
at a tilting Dash 8, "will definitely
not make it, poor bastard,"

and I don't want
to bet against him.

It does make it, straightening
to glide in over the
last of rocks and water
like the pilot actually knows what to do,
like the pilot can hear us, or cares.

"Too high," Scott says, "too high,
he's overshooting,
he'll never stop in time."
And then he does, and we drink,
scraping air with our eyes.

THE RATS OUTSIDE ME

Spines pulled in an inflexible
French curve, all haunch to keep their mouths
at the earth, licking dust,

they are scuttling eggplants, gray-brown from
rot but clean in their fashion,
in the way wet gravel is clean.

I question only the where of them,
their sudden and marvellous attendance,
their subtle rule,

like they've read their own stories, and laughed
well over them, wondering how we have
so completely missed the point of being rat.

Two of them wrestling in an alleyway
on Huron Street, a rat wheel in perpetual motion
until the wall breaks them apart, hissing,

punch drunk they face me,
certain in the direction of events to follow.

And, after visiting Michael for the last time,
I watch one cross Elizabeth Street to the hospital,
heading in to visit the disease.

MOVING DAY

When Jim left Jane;
or the other way —
see Jane kick Jim's ass out the door
see Jim leave —
there was a wine of bitterness
and an empty van
filled, for less than an hour, with:
raw clothes, books and painting after painting,
sketchbooks and rolled paper,
cases of paints and brushes;
a turntable, two televisions,
neither very good, plants,
a toolbox moved too soon to help
with a table saw suddenly too big for
the basement steps
— too late, and the walls suffered.
Four flights of stairs,
and my grandmother in the ground
less than a block from the new place.
A patch of ice
under the sliding side door,
certain to knock one of us
to the cement before it was over.
There was exhaustion and
hunger and pain and recognition;
familiarity, wistfulness, resignation.
There was a van full of the future,
and the same emptied, but for
that damned saw, rattling along Queen St.
after dark, touring our lives
as young men grown tired;
Jim and I and a table saw,
Super Bowl Sunday,
knowing more than we'd ever wanted,
seeing the city,
glad of each other.

HOW MR. EMIGH PICKED UP
A HITCHHIKING IDI AMIN IN UGANDA,
BUT SURVIVED TO TEACH US ALL TO
READ SHAKESPEARE

I always think of them as geese,
or better, swans,
but they must have been some
gawkish African bird,
aimed at from a passing window
in a casual, madman way.

I never asked
if he saved any shell casings, or
if he left them to roll around
the floor of his Volkswagen,
rattling over the pitted roads
like teeth shaken in a jam jar.

DOG PARK

Instruct my legs
to push into gravity.

A park domed in peculiar
ice, and my shoes,
stupid at the surface.

The dogs come back
in the morning, happy
to see themselves
decorating the air.

If I had claws,
I would also
be excited.

BATHURST

It seemed, if you wanted to see it
that way, an hour
all about dying; or dying
that might have happened
but didn't,

me, with a pocket full of negatives;
anti-photos of men you know
camping, drinking,
smoking, holding fish
that might die,
but don't,

the film missing
each crucial release;
each bass, a smudge
wiped and removed from the surface,
back to mystery, men's hands
a bad memory.

Riding north past the park where
Jim's bike was stolen
the second and last time, north
through former beds
and naked struggles,
past Dundas finally, and my former
hospital bed with its view
of the funeral parlour
across the street —

I send a finger to both and ride on

into a memory of near death
that will wake a man cold and still,
make him nervous at crosswalks,

and in strange cities
whose traffic he hasn't yet figured,
but is trying to.
And he might one day wonder
about his mother, certain
decisions she makes,
like the day, with me on my bike,
fish in my pocket,
watching, she took
his hand and threaded traffic,
her car being ticketed
across Bathurst,
his sister in her arms
she lets go of his hand to wave,
yell "wait," to mean "no, I'm here, in the road
with children."

He follows her
around a van, blue, sees
someone waving both arms,
sees only arms
crossing in the air;
everyone expects him to die right there —

his mother, who's dying also,
the parking officer,
who's seen the speeding car
and is waving both arms,
the driver, me, him,
all minds one on the subject of his death.

Instead, he touches
the car's hood,
hot with a day's driving,
breathes rubber and brake,

stands entirely still,
a city expanding
from his forehead, and
lives beyond all expectation,
perpetually nervous, entirely alive.

I will make it home
through traffic, hang my bike
and develop my photos;
fish on hooks, underwater
in a chemical bath, sharpening,
foreign against a background of trees,
bound to live longer;
still swimming,
still swimming.

DOG'S GRAVE UNCOVERED

skin like a blanket on a too-warm night
a rib like the root of that tree
fur like eight mangy squirrels
crossing Queen's Park Crescent
teeth like a dog's teeth
dull yellow when scraped of dirt
ears like old misshapen pancakes
claws like fresh hawthorn
legs like a photo of this dog —

running over grass
after a frisbee it will never
catch but instead just knocks
to the ground with its mouth and
then stumbles over
flipping itself one hundred and eighty
degrees all legs
in the air like these legs now —

eyes like the inside of pockets
a tail like rope half-buried
a smile
a stench like boxes of old potatoes
at the market on Christie Street

A SURE KNOWLEDGE
OF BLOOD

They are stealing wooden
clothes pegs and half-ripe
apples from trees;
surprising no one,
dressed as small, playful Nazis.

guns not bread
They are killing a pig
in an earth cellar beneath the barn,
hiding the meat
from certain neighbours,
draining blood for sausage.

She is a distant aunt
twisting a chicken's neck
in that landscape
of sickly wet fields
and war heat.

A record is playing
behind weary neighbours,
reminding them of heartbeats
and a coarse grain loaf
bread not guns and all
the children in uniform.

She hates Catholics and pears,
and grows to such a size
that generations later the rooms
still taste of potatoes
locked out of the air.

They watch names dissolve
and keep tight to walls;
hooks tear at stomachs
and barns blaze that colour;
they eat fear with blood and
the peppered flesh of fresh-killed pigs.

They will tunnel
through the mid-century
and listen to oceans
try to kill them all
with indifference.

He will emerge walking,
wet and red and stinking,
suddenly brothered
with a dead uncle's shoes,
hoping certain things are forgotten
in a city of corned beef hash.

She will offer
all she has left on the table;
mustardy greens, warm beer
and rabbit meat;
a tuberous, untidy beginning.

DISTRICT OF

All anyone needs to do
to get America, to
really get it,
is to stand solidly just there,
three steps down from Lincoln level
on that giant rectangular rock
on the edge of the Potomac,
edging into vastness — the Atlantic,
a few deep bays and several submarines away —

not looking in the obvious
direction, letting the reflecting pool
reflect your back,
ignoring legislature as an idea,
and monument as hubris,
an adjective slipping into noun
without time to think
of implications; that's just
how sneaky those Americans are.

Stand low three steps
to maintain your station;
stand and know about the golf course
of the dead behind his bearded grimace;
know about deaths by accident;
airplanes bouncing
off bridges, a mystery man sinking
beneath the ice to the adulation of,
well, everyone, because of what he meant,
you see, as much as — more than — who he was.

Those fields of death,
I dare you to evict them
from your head once they've taken residence;
a human mind

is not fashioned to understand
so many white, hollowed-out crosses.

Notice my own death hanging out
just over the water,
toying, setting down,
becoming, maybe, possible; wondering if she
should let that taxi do her business
and knock me down for good,
as I try to cross with my father.

Know that instead the capital
just spins briefly, and
suddenly there is the sound
of helicopters again, and a jogger — a man
so good-looking, so solidly American, gazing
at me and wondering how I am.

Stand and know that here
is the spot where I kissed Monika, where
I had wanted to kiss Alison,
and where I should have
kissed Georgiana if time
ever bothered to work correctly —

you won't forget, of course, about
death by war and assassination,
death by ignorance;
countryman killing countryman
in the dark of history;
you won't forget those things,
but they'll seem less important
when you think about
Georgiana, and then Alison —
chances that don't come back

belong to something other
than stone.

Stand there and know that David
couldn't concentrate
on the big man and his big words —
emancipation, forescore, no —

David just couldn't think
about that stuff, because he had to
piss and couldn't imagine
something as real as a toilet
right there with Jimmy Stewart,
Martin Luther King and
everyone else;

something about his prostate,
though not serious,
thank god, but it sure
made the drive down here an adventure.

Know that, and you'll get it.

SHIMMER & DISAPPEAR

You are the girl who
drifts in and out
of my city

in London,
you confess virginity
on the lower of two
bus levels;
you laugh through
three films in a row
drinking cider from
a tin

in New York,
you never leave
the bridges, any
of them, all of them;
a river wind pushes
through your curls — you are traffic

Toronto is a seat
beneath olive trees in
the spring, for you
and all the men
who make characters of you

and at the western
edge,
in the unnameable Southwest,
you run out
into the desert, hoping
the heat will flatten you
to nothing.

IT IS YOUR CITY

Your city is the edge of something,
and while there should be ocean breezes
and the coolness of mountains,
it is hot and wet in darkness; your
trees bleed water into the street,

and I will ride this bicycle
beneath the branches, gliding through
long, smooth curves,
bleeding wet

because it is dark and
empty of cars, because my speed
is the only coolness

there are stone gates at the intersection
and it will always be this dark

because the smell of lemons
is in the air, flowers I can't know;
it will go on like this for miles

flat and smooth and dark, no
real work for my legs,
and a safety from being alone in it
everyone alone in it, listening
to radios through the night, whispering,
rasping into telephones their tiredness
and tired angers; one man
drives past me, leans
from his window and shouts "puppies;"
he says "puppies" over again
because it works

and when the rain comes
it is a welcome, whitening
mist in the streetlights

because I no longer
have to hold on,
I can lie down on this bicycle
and disappear into this rain
in long smooth curves

because you live in this city,
so how could you be
unprepared for the rain.

HOW WE'LL EXPLAIN IT
TO EACH OTHER

The bench was crushed
by a falling oak, days
after you sat and talked
about nothing important;
the park is a bowl
for snow.

What is the word for
the sound of late autumn
pellets, driven by wind
into the sidewalk
skin of dead leaves?
I should remind you,

I should remind you
of skiers making
tracks on Boulton Avenue,
cars dead and elemental,
practiced and refined and
therefore useless.

There are border corners
in your neighbourhood
and staircases that go nowhere;
reasons not to be here —
past 2-for-1 Pizza,
three strides to the gas station,
a fog of snow on leaves
carries you under
trains, out of sound.

The steps above Spadina
rise to warmth and the smell
of lemon trees, crashing
from the weight of old
winters.

For some reason, only
the thumbs go cold.

What is the word for that?

MY LONGEST RELATIONSHIP

You and I are lovers for the time
it takes fingers to brush the warmth
of a body from cloth;
in that unending interval,
our children graduate
and go on to forget us
in their careers,

we make discoveries
about each other's skin, grow
tired of all the usual crap —

my pointless jealousies;
your unending flirtations.

In the time it takes to grow cold
on a cool night, you and I
hold hands through all the movies,
and worry at each new illness,

you quit smoking for good,
while I never quite do

until I remove my hand from
the small of your back,
none of our friends can remember
the world before us;
we walk together on fifteen percent
of the world's streets —
that's just an estimate,
until I remove my hand

and you slide away on some dance floor,
your bare feet in sand,
your history empty of me.

A deadly physics

DIMENSION

after midnight,
in the light of street lamps,
the front tire of my bicycle
spins backwards

if I ride enough in darkness,
I will never be older than I am

WHAT IF WE FALL OFF?

to make us feel lighter
in terror, booze and night,
Einstein proposes
time is a circle

or

time is a spiral staircase
in need of fresh black paint

on which we ascend and
descend for our amusement

the smoothness of the centre pole
cool against a nervous palm

here and there, we meet
ourselves, and must lean out

against the railing
to let each other pass

THE YELLOW RULE

never accept a ride from friends
of someone you've just left,
no matter how cold the night;
you can't be sure
what they know about you

this rule stands
for one full year after
the last sex

FIRE

as elements go
fire is your least predictable,
readying itself at all times
beneath surfaces
and behind conversations,
like an excuse

it has been known to
interrupt a body
with sudden, uninvited
immolation, usually
in response to fearful thoughts

in other words

those who tremble, thinking
about spontaneous combustion
often combust

stop thinking about it

stop it

PRESSURE

massy, ancient rock will open
itself after successive freezing
and thawing of moisture trapped
away in imperceptible cracks

and

only a finite number
of metaphors can be scratched
from this phenom —
only six very good ones

as

a man who indulges the same
false hope many times
over a few short years
will have physically damaged
the tissues of his heart

this one,
and the six good ones

THE YOWL PRINCIPLE

on Melville Avenue, the night winds
vary in strength
according to the number
of mating cats in the front
yards of my nearest neighbours

gusts enough to move
the shade, and there
will be kittens

A BODY IN MOTION

art contains a mass
greater than that of
the combined mass of
its physical components

for example

the bust of a man
made entirely of green
household sponges,
through the weight of its
stare compounded over
successive long winters,
can crush a small child

WAVE THEORY

a red light at the corner of
Howland and Wells
blinks on and off
once a second

when I am swimming
in a river up north
the light blinks once for
each second I can't breathe,
and when I ride in airplanes
it counts down the time remaining

snow has little effect on it

the 400 series poems

THAT PHOTOGRAPH EXPLAINED

a cute kid with her head through
the seat of an outhouse toilet,
not down into it but up from the hole,
unused yet,
clean as dirt;

wide emptiness walled in
by a suddenness of grasping
tree roots, by severed earthworms

construction of the outhouse

cedar to counter odours,
the rot of building
on impending shit and piss,
arguments about the height of a bench,
where to cut the hole —
the distance between any
given heel and knee
is intellect and assertion

this girl, narrow enough in bones
to be lowered through an opening,
a photograph of her head
rising up from an opened seat,

the tensed
smile of someone
hanging on above
a dark fresh hole

and for some moments
before and after,
while someone older readies the camera,
while a family stands laughing

in a haze of
summer flies, she crouches
in earth, smells
cut cedar, marvels at hiddenness,

how she knew it would feel this cold

CERTAIN TALENTS

Inside amber water,
the river is broken mostly,

crevassed and salted
with centuries-old trunks worn
slippery by persistence
and generations of fish bellies.

Scott swims
           must be
thirty feet below me,
and I watch a rope of air
flick back from his mouth;

how he gets the depth, emptying
his lungs, becoming a miniature

dropping through canyons

a visible patience, his eyes
on the river's skin, calm
like someone who will never die of suffocation.

We are drinking in
a river north of Peterborough;

we drink beer in cans
thrown to us by friends who sit in sunshine.

They talk about houses,
and throw cans when prompted.

Fish-touching, the oiled-leaf
feel of a tail fin across fingers;
another game between us,
after thirty years of play.

Scott is winning because, after
thirty years, he can
still empty his lungs
without fear, can make
of his mind a fish tail slipping off
into coppery darkness.

SMOKES

I recognize one of my bodies
from 1959,
that famous period
of photos and black shoes,

then young Peggy S____
went and married that
good-looking German boy
who owns three suits because
his brother came off the boat a tailor

the ridged thumbnails
of carpentry,
exiting a limousine on
Bloor Street

the more cheese I eat
the more we all eat,
we recognize

he must have been there,
looking west into
the park, maybe smoking

maybe it was too warm
in his black shoes, and
he wanted a drink to ease him
past the ex-wife

that's where war takes you,
to the back rooms
of the hairdresser brothers —
lovers to all Forest Hill,
falling elevators,
a deli on Peter Street
and rabbits hung to cure
from apartment windows

they are midnight raiders
of the new parkway,
shifting the barricades back

sometimes an expression
can't see the hand in front of its face

that's one pack
of cigarettes never finished
being bought, one
gorgeous piece of stuff

SHE'S A GRAND BEND

Scott played a man
with a satchel of money
and some kind of stage gun
to help define the situation.

His theatre lit the air
in soy fields near Lake Huron,
drawing moths like buses.

In the orange evening,
before curtain, I walked a long way
through barley to touch a windmill
and ended up climbing it
in a fog of rust.

Later in dark warmed
like asphalt, I readied
the beer in my trunk, and listened
to blonde actresses laughing
exactly as you'd expect.

Scott said,
It's like none of them
ever saw a real constellation.

CROW

Crows, you notice,
prefer the very tops of trees;
being claustrophobic, a cage
of branches at mid-trunk
would set them panicking.

Born time-wasters, they're
the TV watchers of nature,
enraptured by shiny things.
They perch beside highways,
at the very tops of trees, and
gaze liquidly at the big
river of shiny things, flowing
in two directions at once.

Proud of their own mystery,
they like to show up
just when it seems their shape
against the sky
is most symbolic of —
what? — death, intelligence
in the woods,
laughter let slip into the past.

While you walk your parents' dog
through a winter forest
of bald branches, they appear,
at the very tops of trees, and speak
of their own arrivals, disappearing
just when you settle on
what that pure
throat noise might mean.

EVERYTHING
THAT'S NOT THERE

All the wolves in the wolf factory paused
at noon, for a moment of silence.
– John Ashbery

One
I'm ignoring a button and,
instead, trying to decide:
river or lake?

I'm not anywhere I've ever been, and
the button distracts me,
makes me think of
grandfathers I've known,
that lemony cake they
always serve after funerals.

It's narrow enough to be
a river, but it might
not be moving.
I'm interested in movement,

think about erosion, what that might mean
for the button, and all
the other buttons near me right now.

So, it's a lake – small
but deep, and

I'm listening to newspaper,
waiting for Paul to
finish his assault
on a toilet in some

country-ass gas station in
lilac season,
wondering, as usual, what
it would take to just walk away
right now, down that hill
and into that lake,
leave the car keys for these two
guys I like well enough,
but still, just go…

In Lake Ontario, years
ago, looking for my car keys
with an old girlfriend,
just the right kind of
person to find car keys
on a sandy lake bottom
the size of three countries.

Chambers works that
newspaper like there's
a prize for noise in reading;
he hasn't been disturbed by the sight
of an Orthodox priest
in the donut shop in Newcastle —
like you'd *expect*
to see that in lilac season.

I'm standing
on a riverbank, looking
at my shoes in some pushed-back
mound of solemn dirt,
and there is a button;

all sorts of things are missing;
there's that relationship between

Chambers and the woman
in that book store —
used to be right there somewhere;

used to be
the buttons go missing, and
you live with the suit
anyway — what the hell? — but
now the suit and
everything in it is gone,
and there's that button
between my shoes.

She shows up, out of nothing,
a woman carrying
a child and a face
that makes sense.
It's credible she'd show up
with that face, smiling
and drinking beer in the shade;
back from nothing, out of empty.

Two

In the town of Fergus,
it looks like everything
is made from the same stone,
like there should be a hole in the earth
somewhere the size of Fergus —
all the buildings, bridges,
stairways and public fountains
the same gray stone.

I have to trust memory,
watch my feet
in relation to trees and
the red gravel roadway down
the centre of things

that have achieved
a state of being there
and not being there
at once.

Stand still, look at the chapel
with the dead house behind,
ignore everything that's not there,
remember an angle
and the number of steps,

a feeling of a number of steps,

and pick out the marker,
pebbled black and quartz.

Three

There is no method
of recall, just the waiting
to hear Chambers say something
that lets me know he's found it.
There's that button between my shoes,
and I hope it's not too plain, what he says;
with Chambers you hope
it's never plain, not *here it is*,
or *I found it*, but
bingo, or *yes*,
or something without words;
a nod at the ground
from fifty yards away.

The last time I looked
for my grandmother
I couldn't find her,
walked out a grid, checked
stones back and front,
listened to crows for
silent minutes and became satisfied.

But there's one extra seat
in the back,
that's Paul on the cell
phone and beside him
someone who didn't come,
because even the voice on the phone
will change on this drive;

he will weaken a little and
stalk windy parking lots
trying to squeeze it all,
every last thing, through
the air.

With my mother in a windy parking lot,
a truck bearing down in winter,
and trying to pull words
back into —
what the hey? —
on our way to buy a suit
with extra buttons sewn into
the sleeve;

a book of funeral etiquette,
good for a few laughs
with the kids, before they
bring out the lemon cake.

The voice on
the cell phone, like
a girl with red hair,
someone near rows of hay bales,
who has watched breathing stop;
a voice preparing
for unpleasantries, a wider
vision, some plan
for continuing after the
chipping of sharp hammers,

she listens
to the three of us
get further away, laughing,
and decides
it feels right
to drop him off
where there's laughter.

I agree with the hair,
and maybe with her
smell like hay and lilac.

On the roadside, dead
trunks stand up to the wind
half-drowned in a rippled surface;
there are several moments of
silence before
the phone rings again

in Ottawa, on that bridge
where I hold
the hand of any girl —
just think back and
pick one —
it's all sunshine
and hangovers,
but they're all present
missing, unseen
and watching
like a voice on the telephone.

ONTARIO GOTHIC

she's gone now, so there's an end of it

I am sent for some lost reason, to borrow
something or make an announcement,
the kind of thing a child can't mistake
without trying.

Along the way, there's a sagging plank bridge
spanning the ditch of watercress, bloated frogs, and
bullrush leaves like knife blades in the air around
my eyes; fly-perch Queen Anne's Lace at the far edge, and then
three giant hounds, thick-skulled behind a fence.

She is paring something – this is back when
people still pared – an apple maybe, something
white when revealed, spiralling dull skin to
the counter top, cool darkness defining indoors from out
where lake breezes wither on the shore.

This is the house where fish go to die
and moose are brought in pieces, like lumber
from the woods; she is married to blood and
has brought blood into the world, formed it
for a time into Danny, a son aimed
at stone walls, highway ditches and roadside trees.

He sits and watches me at my job,
bringing something or preparing to take another
thing away, bouncing on my heels, wanting
grass again and a distance from well-oiled rifles
and dry piscine skins on the wall.

She smiles as the knife slips
cleanly through her thumb; outside,
the lake is coughing up more fish for her dinner,

and a failed impulse has me stalled at
the threshold of her kitchen, watching
the apple recoat; she smiles like a
tourist sizing up a snapshot,
no sure protocol for what should happen next.

I cross to the counter, feet heavy with confusion,
and kiss her strong on the mouth, a brown
and tropical mashing of lips, rust-flavoured and tense,
a hopeless gesture tooled by ignorance,
but final and large and angry.

Danny's fingers mark the skin above my elbow
"If you ever kiss my mother again..."
like a red haze of knowing hasn't scarred itself
on me, running the lawn past howling dogs
and pausing to bounce at the centre of the bridge,
to look back and wait for that first crack of doom —

but she's ash now, so, finally, there's an end of it.

PERCH

Unconsciously, I rejoin
the war between all the fish
of the lake and we
few people onshore.

It is a struggle I retired from
young, succeeding
once when only playing at it,
that perch
jerking on the spike-end of
a barbecue skewer,
and me in charge of it.

I have buried that fish in
my mother's garden every year
since then;
slowly the soil becomes
a lake; full of fish,
fed by them
and feeding,

and I remain in charge,
suddenly on my feet in shallow,
yelling through a snorkel,
impossible to make words,
my teeth grinding rubber,

a hollow breath,
emptying out the bottom of my lungs,
screeching for mother,
and that perch
desperately alive and bleeding
down the steel to my hand.

Where had I learned
that lucky flick
of wrist and shoulder?
Caught that perch without a dodge,
caught me winning
and not wanting to,
afraid now of dexterity,

how steel looks
so much cleaner under water.

PENDRITH MINI VARIETY

Paul leaves his Christmas lights
lit through February,
and parks at a slant
to amuse his wife.

There are alleyways
that can turn this city
into a sea port —
masts and flagpoles
from the baseball standards in
Christie Pits;
fish in mist and funk.

Without a living room,
the corner house couple
watch television
in racks of potato chips
and several coolers,
not close enough to touch,
but together and
waiting to be interrupted.

In the event of deliberate
catastrophe, their small store
would continue three days
or less, and Paul
would drive past it,
on his way to the countryside
to release his cats.

SPRING

Out on the frozen lake,
somewhere between a beach and too far
away to see,
there is a brown thing
and a smaller, darker thing
beside it,
like a seated man
and his small, black dog
lying near him —
except, they've been there a week —
garbage, most likely,
ice-hut refuse, left to
find its way to the lake bottom
after all the huts have slid back to shore —
their true homes,
nine months in leafy seclusion
disturbed only for ninety short days
and long nights of brilliant sky and distance.

Ten minutes of nervous
ice-walking brings them no closer,
and the slow heave of a lake's
skin cancels ambition.
Whatever they are, out there
beyond binoculars, they're alone,
but for each other,
unknown, waiting for spring.

MORNING ON LAKE SIMCOE

There are many left behind, awake,
aware of me,
who have stopped at a window
to notice the boat, wonder
how long it's been here,
if I've caught anything,
if I need help.

I'm alone, away out
past the line in the water
where shore flattens against the sky,
becomes a photograph of itself,
becomes scenery, and the lake
a gentle, overturned bowl.

I'm out beyond most sounds, the
water calm as a street, flat,
empty; it gives nothing.

I am watching
the land take on light,
my mother asleep behind her small window
another hour;
my father has found me
in binoculars, muttered
something predictable, lost
and found me again.

He's thinking about the morning,
about the timing of breakfast,
about how much dog crap
there always is on the lawn,
about sons, the mystery
of them suddenly becoming
larger, moving around him,

taking his breakfast, drawing children
to him from across the road, floating
on morning, so far out,
away out beyond sounds,
beyond the lawn.

I stopped casting an hour ago;
some mornings
there's no point; the water's
surface hard-packed, shoving
me into the sky; not so much
floating as rejected, pushed
back into what I breathe, and
every conversation I try
to have, man to fish, goes nowhere.

I lean my spine against
the bow, watch
my father watch me, and
wait for that small window to open.

BECKY'S BACKWARD DIVE

There is the matter
of her fingers,
splitting into something
less than perfect;
a lake like oil on air.

How many mosquitoes
have sipped her
late afternoon light,
her spine worn
with persistence?

And still,

her toes leave the
dockwood
wanting more.

SMELT

You hang a light
from a pole
to fake the moon,
turn them off course
and lead them into
shallows they'd avoid
given a choice.

Mostly you hang the light
because it works,
because smelt can't choose,
won't discern when the moon
signals life
and when it draws a net.

Everyone knows
a moth will slam
itself against hot glass
until it dies of light,

and every year, the
same April moon draws
a group of men north
along the highway,
generations of their family
meeting generations of mine,
for a few nights each year.

Grandfathers first,
when the trip was longer
because cars and roads were younger,
the Italian men slept in canvas
tents, wet with breathing
beside my grandfather's cabin,
a wooden slat box just

inside the unlocked screen door
full of vegetables from their
market downtown, bottles
of last year's wine
on the steps, rained on
or sweating with frost dew,

and the smelt ran
for three nights straight,
the same three nights each year.

The lake was darker then,
the trees thicker,
and they talked for over
an hour when he finally
ran hydro to the place,
talked about the two
lightbulbs, and how many
moths there suddenly were,
their lanterns on poles
bringing the shoreline to boil,
more smelt than water after
a while, tiny bodies
stretching the nets,

wine and shouting,
and my grandfather
wading in to help them
haul the load.

A generation later came
the neighbour, Mr. Lough,
and the scientific method,
me on the rocks
beside the beach, watching,
my grandfather retired

from the nets, and
the Italian men moving next door
to comfortable chairs
in the boathouse, fire in
the oil drum, and every year
a new system,

every year fish like prairie wheat,
fish like simmering rice,
fish like hordes of life trying
to swim to the moon.

Tonight, we step from the car
to find a small group
of laughing men
under the trees, young men
wondering how, and old men
to make it happen,
still with their wine and
vegetables, who remember

my grandfather like I never knew him,
young and thin
and not bothered by cold water.

They know where the lights hang
in the shed; they light
the fire and spread
the nets,

faking the moon,

but the lake hasn't boiled in years,
and we could all lose patience,
could stop briefly
knowing each other.

SUMACH

Many nights entire
in one, and no motive
to choose between them,
and say that was the night when...

Stan leaned, a half-man
in shadow by the side door,
comfortable, on brick
and asphalt, weedy sumach
overtop;
his face a friendly mystery,
shading in and out
with the breeze.

Mimi walked past us, wrapped
in dusk and her marriage,
never raising her eyes
to the two of us, opposite her,
recognizing and silent, noticing
how wide the demarcation.

The party was quieter
than expected; everyone
as tired as everyone else, or
just wondering
about the possibility of such a
September evening, dark
and warm, covered over
with a weighty calm.

The apartment was new
to us all, more
comfortable than we could have
reasonably expected –
and, in the corner, a half-finished portrait
watching and not judging.

That was the night when...

We learned about Al's lungs,
and rebellion in the body,
and what it might eventually be like
for us all; Stan in shadows,
Mimi heading for her porch,
Paul with his cane
and paintbrushes, letters framed
like landscapes where he sleeps.

We watched Paul hug Dennis,
thirty years apart
from identical lives,
that warm breeze from the sumach
slipping between them,
that night when...

Alexandra, just drunk enough,
removed her clothes
and slipped, laughing, into
the bathtub; a prize
everyone had won
for staying late, for staying awake,
for wanting
her free, or just wanting her.

That night
we left early,
and went home to sleep.

SUMMER AT ORO

There is nothing up my sleeve,
but a 1942 Grundig
mantle radio with Bakelite
knobs, the kind
with brown ridges
around the sphere of them,
and hundreds of catches
inside the mechanism
to make you feel you're
affecting something when
you turn and search a frequency.

Someone's father, maybe mine,
once found five dollars
in the back of an
old radio —
when he removed the drilled board
to get at the tubes, there,
an old Canadian fiver with
a very young Queen.

But there is nothing up my
sleeve except an old radio —
1942, check the date —
and Grundig; doesn't that just
sound so German?

Once, it impersonated
dictators, and later taught me
to watch baseball on a night ceiling
near the lake,
my crazy aunt with a yellow
flower drawn around her navel
listening, somewhere near,
and repeating names to me —

Buck Martinez, Rance Mulliniks —
my radio speaks so many languages.

There was the fiver, and
my father — doesn't he just sound
so German?

My aunt told him
ask me why I get up in the morning
ask me
and my father, still immigrating,
why?
waiting for the joke:
I was hoping you'd know.

My father spent the fiver on beer,
a sweaty case of short brown bottles
cool in the hedge
to share with his brothers
while they spoke German at each other,
one bottle missing,

my first beer, hidden
up my sleeve.

MINNOW

My father will gut a fish
slowly, watch the nerve
firings, the slow twigging,
feel the muscle contract,
and always tell himself
there's no pain,
the club has done its work
in the boat, and what
we see is
meat and electricity.

He will pull at the stomach
with his finger, feel
for anything interesting, slice
the good ones with a knife-tip,
reveal whole crayfish,
leeches rolled in on themselves,
and other fish —
miniatures of the kill.

There are times
these small fish also move;
lessons in chronology
that have me running to the dock,
stomach minnow in hand,
wondering.

MY ISLAND

I have lived on an island
too long,
walked too many beaches
and counted far
too many waves.

I have looked at the city
like a photo of itself,
across the water,
alive with friends,
and have turned my back,
seeking gulls.

I have taught the walls
of my small room to ask,
Where is your wife?
Where are your children?
I have heard children in the trees.

This red bicycle hurts me now —
I look at the city
and think,
fall on top of me now,
bring all the bricks down on me,
I'm ready now.

Acknowledgements

I would like to thank the City of Toronto through the Toronto Arts Council for the grant I received during the writing of this book, and the Province of Ontario through the Ontario Arts Council for past support of my writing.

I would also like to thank Toronto Artscape and the Gibraltar Point Artist Residency Program for providing me with residence and studio space on Toronto Island for the month of October 2001. The time and atmosphere so generously provided were instrumental to the completion of this book.

Thanks to the editors of the following literary magazines, websites and anthologies where earlier versions of some of these poems appeared: *The Fiddlehead, TickleAce, The Literary Review of Canada, thedrunkenboat.com, Taddle Creek Magazine* and *taddlecreekmag.com, Queen Street Quarterly, The Antigonish Review*, and *The IV Lounge Reader*.

Special thanks to Beth Follett, owner, operator and publisher of Pedlar Press for much gentle pushing and support, to Zab for her perfect eye, and to my editor, Kevin Connolly, for his large brain and for making the book better without making me cry.

Thank you to poets Chris Chambers and Claudia Dey for close readings of early drafts and invaluable poetic advice, and to all my fellow Gibraltar Point artists for music and whiskey.

Finally, special thanks to my wife Georgiana Uhlyarik, and to the 400 series people: Stephen Degen and Julia Gerlach; Fred K. Stephenson, Marjorie Stephenson and Susan Woollings Stephenson; Hartwig and Amanda Degen; Danny, Warren and Audrey Lough; Ken, Helen, Brad, Ted and Sue Stephenson; Günther and Lore Degen, Hauke Degen, Patricia Degen; Belva Hughes, Theresa and Paul Ortiz, Margot and Edwin Hastbacka; and Scott Watson.

John Degen's first collection of poems, *Animal Life in Bucharest* (Pedlar Press, 2000), received strong critical praise in the national literary press. He has written three scripts for the stage and has recently completed a novel about hockey and backgammon, set in Toronto and Romania. He is also an occasional contributor to a number of Canadian magazines. He lives in Toronto with his wife, Georgiana, and twin sons, Fred and Jacob.